"Resilience in Motion: How Fitness and Faith Helped Me Overcome Cancer" by

Shyam Thakker

TABLE OF CONTENTS

- Chapter 1: The Unexpected Diagnosis

- Chapter 2: The Days to Follow

- Chapter 3: The Surgery

- Chapter 4: Recovery and Rehabilitation

- Chapter 5: The Road to Recovery

- Chapter 6: Returning to Life

- Chapter 7: Reflections and Lessons Learned

- Chapter 8: A New Chapter Unfolds

- Chapter 9: Pay It Forward

- Chapter 10: The Future is Bright & Conclusion

- Pictures & Thank you

DEDICATION

Dedicated to my loving family and friends, whose unwavering support, unconditional love, and unrelenting encouragement carried me through the darkest days and brightest triumphs. Without you, I wouldn't have made it. Thank you for being my rock, my safe haven, and my everything. And to my students, who inspire me every day with their resilience and determination. And to everyone who has ever faced adversity, may my story be a reminder that hope, faith, and courage can overcome even the toughest challenges.

BIOGRAPHY

Shyam Thakker (Desiboy) is a cancer survivor, dance fitness instructor, inspiring speaker, educator, behavior specialist, and entrepreneur who has overcome incredible odds to share his story with the world. Born and raised in Kenya, Shyam grew up with a passion for dance, fitness, and helping others. As an esteemed educator and behavior specialist at Dearborn Public Schools in Michigan, he has dedicated their career to supporting students with special needs, earning him the prestigious title of #1 Educator in North America 2021. His remarkable work has been recognized with a personal letter of commendation from the White House. When not inspiring young minds, Shyam, also popularly known as Desiboy, teaches dance fitness classes at Life Time and has founded Desiboy Fitness, his own online nutrition supplement business, built on his passion for wellness and empowerment. With a career spanning over 20 years, he has inspired countless students, clients, and community members with his energy, enthusiasm, and dedication. When faced with colon cancer, Shyam drew upon his strength, faith, and support system to fight back and win. His memoir is a testament to his resilience and a tribute to the power of hope and determination. Shyam

Thakker resides in Canton, Michigan, where he continues to teach, inspire, and live life to the fullest, touching hearts and lives across generations.

INTRODUCTION

In this heart-wrenching and inspiring memoir, Shyam Thakker, also known as Desiboy, shares his courageous battle against colon cancer. With unflinching honesty, he recounts the darkest moments of his journey, but also the resilience, hope, and determination that fueled his fight. From the depths of despair to the triumph of recovery, this book is a testament to the power of the human spirit. With the support of his family, friends, loved ones and the strength of their faith, Shyam refused to give up, and his story will inspire you to do the same. A riveting and uplifting read, this book is a reminder that no matter what life throws our way, we have the capacity to overcome, to heal, and to thrive.

Chapter 1: **The Unexpected Diagnosis**

Thursday, February 22nd 2024 started like any other day, but it would become a turning point in my life. I woke up with a swollen and painful left calf, which I initially attributed to a muscle pull from teaching my fitness classes. However, as the days passed, the swelling and pain worsened, prompting me to seek medical attention.

After a series of tests and referrals, I was diagnosed with three blood clots in my left calf on Monday, February 26th 2024. The vein specialist put me on a blood thinner, and within three days, the swelling and pain subsided. But little did I know, this was only the beginning of my journey.

As the days went by, I struggled with shortness of breath and a racing heart, which led to a series of tests and ultimately, a devastating diagnosis: a 9cm mass in my transverse colon, confirmed to be cancerous. The news was crushing, but I was determined to fight, surrounded by the love and support of my family, friends, and community.

"February 22nd, a day like any other,

Until pain and swelling made my calf a bother.

Muscle pull, I thought, but days went by,

And tests revealed blood clots, a surprise to the eye.

Relief came with treatment, but new symptoms arose,

Shortness of breath, a racing heart, and anxious sighs.

More tests, more waiting, until the devastating blow,

A cancerous mass, 9cm, in my colon, did grow.

Crushing news, but love and support surrounded me,

Family, friends, and community, a strength to be free.

Determined to fight, I stood, though shaken and worn,

A journey begun, with courage as my dawn."

Chapter 2: **The Days to follow**

The days that followed the diagnosis were a blur of emotions, tests, and uncertainty. I struggled to come to terms with the fact that I had cancer. "How could this be?" I thought. "I'm young and only 51 years old. I'm healthy, I exercise regularly, I eat well." But the truth was, I had a 9cm mass in my transverse colon, and it was cancerous.

The emotional rollercoaster was intense. I felt denial, anger, sadness, and fear all at once. I cried, I screamed, I questioned everything. But amidst all the chaos, I found solace in my loved ones. My family, my friends, my community - everyone rallied around me, offering support, love, and encouragement.

My daughter Meera was my rock, my strength. She stayed by my side through every test, every doctor's visit, every moment of uncertainty. My sister Sima, brother in law

Ashit and my nieces Ami and Sonam flew in from the UK to be with me. My grandniece Pari's innocent smile and laughter brought me joy in the darkest of times. My cousin Radhika Thakker-Damani also flew in from Calgary and was a big moral support in my battle with cancer. My parents, Pradip and Renuka, were my pillars of strength, always there to offer a listening ear and a comforting embrace. Lucas O'Brien was also such a huge support not only for me, but also for my daughter Meera, and my family. And lastly, I cannot forget Manish Nathwani who constantly checked in on me to make sure I was doing well, as did my family from Kenya, Tanzania, Sweden, Canada, UK, and the US.

And then there were my friends, Basma and Nicole - my angels, my confidantes, my partners in crime. They stood by me through every up and down, every triumph and every setback. Together, we laughed, we cried, we prayed, and we fought.

"In the darkness of diagnosis, I searched for the light,

A 9cm mass, a cancerous sight.

Emotions swirled, a rollercoaster ride,

Denial, anger, sadness, fear, I couldn't hide.

But then I found solace, a love so true,

In family, friends, and community, who saw me through.

My daughter Meera, my rock, my guiding star,

My sister, nieces, and cousins, near and far.

My grandniece Pari's smile, a beacon of hope,

My parents' embrace, a shelter from the scope.

Basma and Nicole, friends who stood as one,

Together we faced the battle, under the sun.

In the chaos, I found strength, a will to fight,

A support system, shining bright and light.

Love and encouragement, a powerful grace,

Helping me rise, leaving fear and doubt in its place."

Chapter 3: **The Surgery**

The six-week wait for surgery was agonizing. I felt like I was in limbo, unsure of what the future held. Dr. Asai's words echoed in my mind: "We need to remove 75% of your colon to ensure no stoma bag." The thought of such a significant portion of my colon being removed terrified me. I feared losing my independence, my lifestyle, and my passion for dancing and teaching. The uncertainty threatened my job and my identity.

Despite my fears, I tried to stay active and maintain my physical strength, hoping it would somehow improve my chances of a smooth recovery. But the emotional toll was immense. I felt like I was drowning in anxiety, worry, and fear. I just wanted the surgery over with, to finally have some answers and a chance to start healing.

Finally, the day of the surgery arrived. I was nervous but ready to get it over with. Dr. Asai and her team were reassuring, and I put my trust in them. The surgery was a success, and the mass was removed. Thankfully only 30% of my colon needed to be removed. I spent 14 days in the hospital, recovering and dealing with post-op complications. But I was determined to get back on my feet, literally.

With the support of my family, friends, and medical team, I started my journey to recovery. My primary care physician was instrumental in my care and I am extremely thankful for everything she did, and continues to do for me. Physical therapy, pain management, and a lot of rest were my priorities. And, of course, plenty of prayers and positive vibes from everyone around me.

"In limbo, I waited, six long weeks of fear,

Uncertainty gripped me, tears I couldn't clear.

Dr. Asai's words echoed, a daunting task ahead,

30% & not 75% of my colon, a sacrifice to be made.

Fears of loss and change, they swirled in my mind,

Independence, lifestyle, passion, all left behind.

But still, I held on tight, to hope and to might,

I stayed active, strong, and prayed for a brighter light.

Anxiety and worry, they threatened to consume,

But I faced them head-on, with a heart that refused to succumb.

The day of surgery arrived, I took a deep breath in,

Ready to face the unknown, and let the healing begin.

Dr. Asai and her team, a reassuring embrace,

I put my trust in them, and let their expertise guide me to a safe place.

The surgery was a success, the mass was gone at last,

A new chapter unfolded, as I began my journey to recovery at last.

With family, friends, and medical team by my side,

I took small steps forward, with a heart full of pride.

Physical therapy, pain management, and rest,

A journey to healing, with love and support, I was
blessed.

Keep moving forward, that's what I told myself,

And with each small victory, my strength and hope
were reborn"

Chapter 4: **Recovery and Rehabilitation**

The days following the surgery were a blur of pain management, medication, and rest. I was grateful for the support of my family, friends, and medical team. Dr. Asai and her team checked on me regularly, monitoring my progress and addressing any concerns.

As I slowly regained my strength, I began to realize the magnitude of my journey. I had faced cancer, surgery, and the uncertainty of my future. But I was determined to not let it define me. I wanted to dance again, teach again, and live life to the fullest.

As I began physical therapy, I was determined to push beyond the initial goal of 4 laps around the hospital floor. I set my sights on 6 laps, and by the time I was released from the hospital, I was doing 25 laps, driven by my resolve to win this battle.

My loved ones were my rock, never leaving my side, and their unwavering support inspired me to keep going. I even inspired other patients on the same floor with my determination. However, it was frustrating to confront the physical limitations that prevented me from being myself and doing things I once took for granted.

Without the option of morphine or narcotics due to allergies, I relied on over-the-counter pain medications and sheer willpower to tolerate the pain. I kept moving, refusing to let anything stand in my way. My mantra became "I can do this. I can beat this."

After being released from the hospital, I continued walking around my house and subdivision, following up with my doctors and adhering to their instructions. My primary care doctor, Dr. Hina Syed, was instrumental in my recovery and follow-up care. My family and friends provided invaluable support, and I eventually worked up to walking 7 miles a day, staying active and motivated.

The restriction on lifting more than 10 lbs. for 6 weeks was frustrating, but I knew it was temporary, and my ultimate goal kept me motivated. I was determined to regain my strength and return to my normal life.

"In the aftermath of surgery, I faced pain and fear,

But with loved ones by my side, I found the strength to persevere.

Dr. Asai and her team, a constant guiding light,

Monitoring my progress, banishing the dark of night.

As I regained my strength, my determination grew,

To dance again, teach again, and live life anew.

Physical therapy, a challenge I embraced,

Pushing beyond limits, my resolve left no trace.

From 4 laps to 25, my willpower took the lead,

Inspiring others, my determination did proceed.

Without morphine or narcotics, I relied on my might,

Over-the-counter meds and sheer will, my pain to fight.

My mantra echoed loud, "I can do this, I can beat this"

Refusing to let limitations define my spirit's grit.

Released from the hospital, I continued on my way,

Walking, following up, and adhering to my doctors'

way,

Dr. Hina Syed, a primary care doctor true.

Instrumental in my recovery, her care saw me through.

Family and friends, a support system strong,

Together we walked, 7 miles a day, all day long.

The restriction on lifting, a temporary test,

But my ultimate goal kept me motivated, I did my best.

Regaining strength, returning to life's embrace,

Determined to win, I found my inner grace."

Chapter 5: **The Road to Recovery**

As I continued my physical therapy and rehabilitation, I began to notice small victories along the way. I could walk a little farther, stand a little longer, and even start doing some light stretching. It was a slow and painful process, but I was determined to get back to my normal life.

I remember the first time I was able to walk around my entire neighborhood without needing to rest. It was a small accomplishment, but it felt like a major milestone. I celebrated by doing a little dance in my living room, much to the amusement of my family.

As I progressed, I started incorporating more activities into my routine. I began doing light resistance band workouts, started incorporating various movements, and even some light weightlifting. It was amazing how much strength and flexibility I had lost, but I was determined to get it back.

My loved ones continued to be my rock, supporting me every step of the way. My friends would come over and visit me or would constantly call me to check up on my progress, and my family would cheer me on from the sidelines.

"Small victories, oh so sweet,

A little farther, a little longer to stand and meet.

The pain subsides, progress takes its place,

A slow and steady journey, a triumphant embrace.

The first neighborhood walk, a milestone achieved,

A dance in the living room, joy unsealed and relieved.

Family laughter and cheer, a heart full of delight,

A celebration of strength, a spirit taking flight.

Resistance bands and movements, a new path unfolds,

Light weightlifting, a testament to a will of gold.

Lost strength and flexibility, slowly regained with might,

A determination to rise, shining brighter with each new light.

Loved ones, a constant presence, a support system true,

Friends and family, cheering me on, seeing me through.

Visits, calls, and encouragement, a heart that's full and blessed,

A journey of resilience, a spirit that's truly blessed."

Chapter 6: **Returning to Life**

As my physical strength returned, I began to reengage with the world around me. I started teaching Zumba and Bollywood Dance classes again, gradually increasing the intensity and duration. My students were supportive and encouraging, and it felt amazing to be back in the studio.

I started modifying my routines to accommodate my ongoing recovery. It was a challenge, but I was determined to share my passion for fitness with others.

My social life also began to flourish again. I started attending events and gatherings, reconnecting with friends and family. I even started going to movies and out to dinner with my family.

Throughout this journey, I learned the importance of self-care and prioritizing my own needs. I continued to practice breathing techniques and meditation, finding solace in the peace and calm they brought.

"Strength renewed, I stepped back into the fray,

Teaching Zumba and Bollywood, my passion on display.

Students supportive, encouraging me along,

Back in the studio, my heart sang a happy song.

Modifying routines, accommodating my pace,

Determined to share fitness, a passion that embraced.

My social life blossomed, events and gatherings galore,

Reconnecting with loved ones, making memories once more.

Movies and dinner outings, family time so sweet,

Laughter and joy, a heart that skipped a beat.

Self-care and meditation, a priority I made,

Breathing techniques, peace and calm, a soul that's not frayed.

Through this journey, I learned to prioritize my needs,

Embracing self-care, a vital part of my healing deeds.

Finding solace in peace, a heart that's full and light,

A renewed sense of purpose, shining with all my might"

Chapter 7: **Reflections and Lessons Learned**

As I looked back on my journey, I realized that cancer had taught me valuable lessons. I learned to appreciate the little things, to cherish every moment, and to never take life for granted. I learned to be stronger, braver, and more resilient than I ever thought possible.

I also learned the importance of self-care, prioritizing my own needs, and seeking help when necessary. I discovered the power of mindfulness, meditation, and yoga in healing and growth.

Most importantly, I learned that I was not alone. I had the support of loved ones, friends, and a community that rallied around me. I learned to accept help, to ask for support, and to lean on others when needed.

As I reflected on my journey, I realized that cancer had changed me in profound ways. It had stripped me of my fears, my doubts, and my limitations. It had given me a new perspective, a new purpose, and a new appreciation for life.

"Cancer's lessons, valuable and true,

Appreciate the little things, cherish every moment anew.

Strength, bravery, resilience, I found within,

Never taking life for granted, a heart that's grateful to win.

Self-care, prioritized, seeking help when needed most,

Mindfulness, meditation, yoga, a healing soul to boast.

Not alone, loved ones, friends, and community by my side,

Accepting help, asking for support, a heart that's open wide.

Reflections on my journey, profound changes I've made,

Fears, doubts, limitations, stripped away, a new path

I've paved.

New perspective, purpose, appreciation for life's grace,

Cancer's lessons, a transformation, a new chapter in its

place"

Chapter 8: **A New Chapter Unfolds**

As I continued on my journey, I began to realize that cancer had given me a rare gift - a second chance at life. I was determined to make the most of it, to live life to the fullest, and to pursue my passions with purpose and meaning.

But my journey was not without its new challenges. I had also been diagnosed with Lynch Syndrome, a genetic disorder that increases the risk of developing certain cancers. I knew that this would require regular testing and monitoring, but I was determined to face this new hurdle head-on.

For now, I was choosing to celebrate my victory over colon cancer. I had overcome a major obstacle, and I was proud of myself for my strength and resilience. I knew that I would continue to face challenges in the future, but I was ready to tackle them one day at a time.

But most importantly, I began to share my story, to inspire and encourage others who were facing their own challenges. I wanted to show others that they too could overcome adversity, that they too could find strength in their struggles.

"A second chance at life, a rare gift indeed,

Determined to live fully, passions pursued with purpose and speed.

But new challenges arose, Lynch Syndrome's testing fate,

Regular monitoring, a new hurdle to navigate and abate.

Celebrating victory, colon cancer overcome,

Strength and resilience, a heart that's proud and won.

Future challenges await, but I'm ready to face,

One day at a time, with courage and grace.

Most importantly, my story I began to share,

Inspiring and encouraging others, showing I care.

Overcoming adversity, strength in struggles found,

A beacon of hope, for others to rise above their ground"

Chapter 9: **Paying It Forward**

As I continue on my journey, I feel a strong desire to inspire and motivate others through my story. I aim to become a motivational speaker, sharing my experiences and insights with audiences everywhere. I want to show people that even in the darkest moments, there is always hope and a way forward.

I also feel a deep connection to those who are currently facing cancer and Lynch Syndrome. I want to visit hospitals and support groups, offering guidance, advice, and a listening ear to those who need it. I believe that by sharing my story, I can help others feel less alone and more empowered to face their own challenges.

Furthermore, I am passionate about advocating for cancer awareness and the importance of testing. I want to spread the word about the significance of early detection and the impact it can have on treatment and recovery. I also want to emphasize the importance of living a healthy lifestyle, including regular exercise, balanced eating, and mental well-being.

"A desire burns within, to inspire and motivate,

Sharing my story, a beacon to navigate.

From darkness to hope, a way forward to show,

Motivational speaking, my passion to glow.

Connecting with those, in cancer's grasp,

Support groups and hospitals, a listening ear to clasp.

Guidance and advice, a helping hand to lend,

Empowering others, to face their challenges and mend.

Sharing my story, to ease the feeling of alone,

Empowering others, to find strength in their own.

Advocating for awareness, testing's vital role,

Early detection's impact, on treatment and soul.

Healthy lifestyle, a message to share,

Regular exercise, balanced eating, mental well-being to spare.

Spreading the word, a mission to fulfill,

Inspiring others, to live life to the fullest still"

Chapter 10: **The Future Is Bright**

As I look to the future, I am filled with hope and excitement. I know that I still have challenges ahead, but I am ready to face them head-on. I am proud of the person I have become and the strength I have discovered within myself. I envision a future where I continue to inspire and motivate others through my speaking and advocacy work. I see myself traveling the world, sharing my story with diverse audiences, and making a meaningful impact on people's lives. I also see myself continuing to prioritize my health and wellness, taking care of my body and mind, and living life to the fullest. I imagine myself pursuing new hobbies and interests, nurturing meaningful relationships, and finding joy in everyday moments.

Most importantly, I see myself living a life that is true to who I am, a life that reflects my values and passions. I am excited to see what the future holds, knowing that I have the strength and resilience to overcome any obstacle that comes my way.

"Hope and excitement, a future bright,

Challenges ahead, but I'm ready to take flight.

Proud of the person I've become, strong and true,

Inspiring others, my mission, to see them through.

A world of possibilities, my vision to share,

Traveling far, my story to spare.

Meaningful impact, on lives I'll make my mark,

Prioritizing health, wellness, and joy in every spark.

New hobbies and interests, relationships that thrive,

Living life authentically, my values to survive.

Resilience and strength, to overcome any test,

A future that's bright, and a heart that's at its best"

CONCLUSION

As I reflect on my journey through colon cancer, I am reminded of the power of resilience, determination, and support. From diagnosis to recovery, I have learned valuable lessons that I hope will inspire and empower others facing similar challenges. Through my experience, I have come to understand the importance of:

- **Early detection and regular cancer screening**
- **Keeping up with doctor appointments and medical care - Prioritizing physical and mental well-being**
- **Surrounding oneself with love, support, and encouragement**
- **Embracing hope, positivity, and faith - Advocating for oneself and one's health**
- **Paying it forward and helping others.**

I hope that my story will encourage readers to take control of their health, cherish life's precious moments, and never give up in the face of adversity.

Remember, health is a journey, not a destination. Let us strive to live life to the fullest, cherish every moment, and support one another along the way.

Nothing is Possible Without Prayers & The Unconditional Love and Support from Loved Ones

My amazing Parents Pradip Thakker and Renuka Thakker & my beautiful daughter Meera Thakker

"Family is not an important thing. It's everything." –Michael J. Fox

With my lovely sister Sima, daughter Meera, and amazing
parents Pradip & Renuka Thakker

*"Families are the compass that guides us.
They are the inspiration to reach great
heights, and our comfort when we
occasionally falter."* —Brad Henry

Post-Surgery Lake time with my sister Sima

"Sweet is the voice of a sister in the season of sorrow." —Benjamin Disraeli

My beautiful parents Renuka & Pradip Thakker. I Love
You so much.

**"Nobody on earth can ever love you more
than your parents." – Unknown**

My Amaznig Cousin Radhika Thakker-Damani

"In the cookies of life, sisters are the chocolate chips." —Unknown

With the Family at Cups n Chai. Thank you, Noman.

"Family and friendships are two of the greatest facilitators of happiness." —
John C. Maxwell

My Beautiful Niece Ami from the UK and I enjoying
special moments together.

*"Your presence in my life is a gift that I
treasure every day – being your uncle is a
privilege I hold dear."*

My Amazing Niece Sonam from the UK and I discussing Life.

"The bond between a niece and her uncle is unique, a blend of friendship, mentorship, and familial love that endures."

London Family with the Liverpool FC Flex. Most of them came to the USA to support me and my family & I am forever grateful.

"When trouble comes, it's your family that supports you." –Guy Lafleur

My superman, my father Pradip Thakker

"There is no friendship, no love, like that of the parent for the child." – Henry Ward Beecher

My mother the superwoman, Renuka Thakker

**"A mother's love is the anchor
that keeps us steady in the storm"**

My ROCK STAR and My Best Friend. My
Daughter Meera Thakker

*"No one in this world can love a girl more
than her father."* — *Michael Ratnadeepak*

Always there to support me no matter what. My best
friend, my daughter Meera.

*"Go on, take on this whole world / But to
me you know you'll always be / My little
girl." — Tim McGraw*

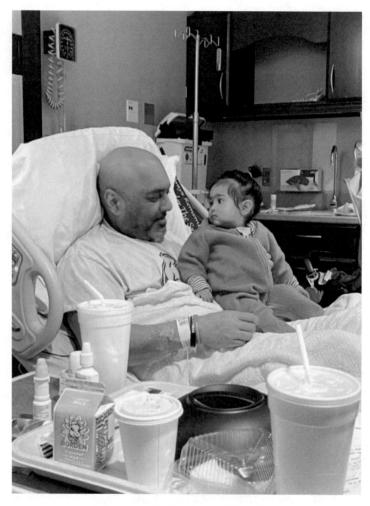

My Angel, Pari Pankhaniya

"Do you ever look at your child and just smile? Not because your child did something amazing, just smiling because you know how blessed you really are."

This pic with my angel Pari Pankhaniya is Priceless

"See the stars? I made a wish on one, and I got you." – unknown

Best Friends Basma & Nicole

With my support and friendship family squad (Basma,
Nicole, Meera, & Lucas

With some of my Life Time Squad on Fox 2 News. The
place when I first revealed that I had Colon Cancer.
(Kiana, Jharni, Robin, Basma, & Akila)

**"Friendship is the only cement that will
ever hold the world
together." Woodrow Wilson**

With some of my Life Time Family & Friends

"Tough times never last, but tough people do" — Robert Schuller

The Support and Uplifting Prayers and
Messages from Loved Ones

A Motivational message from my daughter Meera

"It's not whether you get knocked down, it's whether you get up." – Vince Lombardi

Mom, my cousin Radhika, daughter Meera, & sister Sima waiting and staying positive at the Hospital.

"Alone, you are strong, but together, you'll be stronger than ever." – Unknown

My Dad & Brother in Law taking a nap while I was in surgery for nearly 5 hours.

"In time of test, family is best." — Burmese Proverb

My Primary Care Physician, Dr. Hina Syed, MD (Henry Ford Health) who was ever so instrumental in my care.

"Thank you for your outstanding dedication and care. Your compassion and kindness have made a real difference in my recovery."

The BEST SURGEON who I am so thankful for. The one and only, Dr. Megumi Asai, MD (Colon & Rectal Surgery, Henry Ford Health)

"Thank you so much for the great care and surgery you performed on me. You and your staff have made such a huge difference for me."

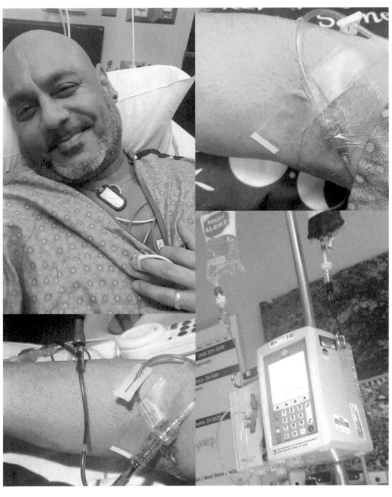

Blood and Iron Transfusion as a result of Anemia due to severe Iron Deficiency & very low Hemoglobin.

"You can be a victim of cancer or a survivor of cancer. It's a mindset." –
Dave Pelzer

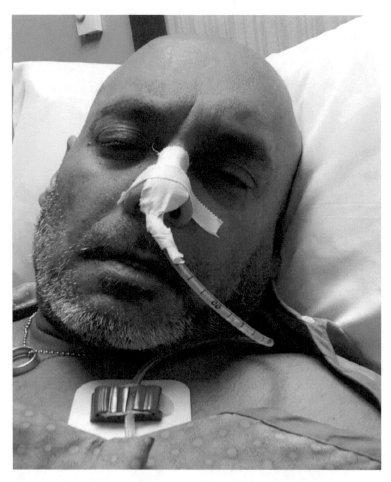

When things did not look too good and I was in a lot of pain. One of the hardest things I had to endure was not being able to take strong pain meds due to allergies.

**"We have two options, medically and emotionally: give in or fight like hell." –
Lance Armstrong**

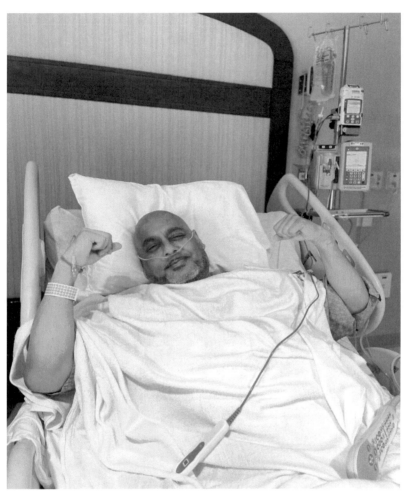

Staying Positive and always trying to smile.

"I think I can. I think I can. I think I can. I know I can." —Watty Piper, The Little Engine That Could

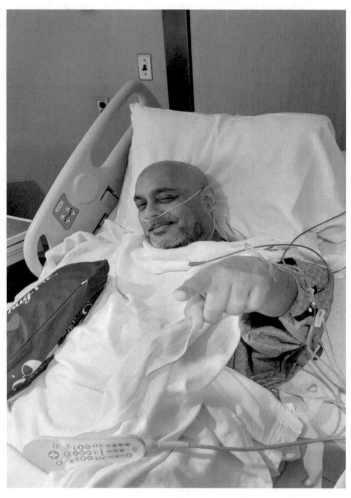

Hugging my fav pillow and trying to do my pose.

"Believe you can and you're halfway there." —Theodore Roosevelt

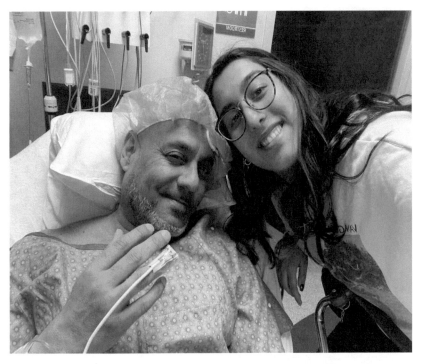

My daughter Meera was always by my side. The reason I had to win this battle.

"One word of encouragement can be enough to spark someone's motivation to continue with a difficult challenge." – Roy T. Bennett

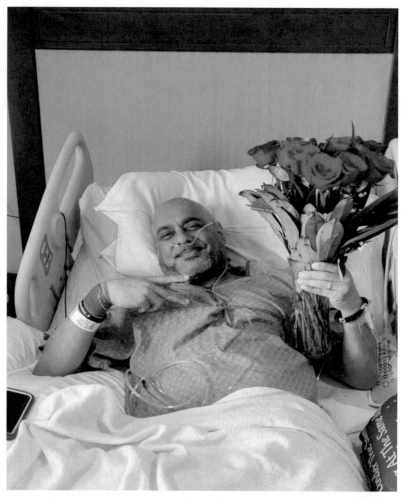

Being showered with love and helping me stay strong.

"Each day is a gift. That is why they call it "present." – Eleanor Roosevelt

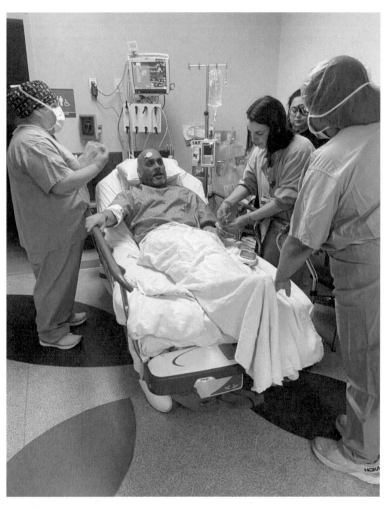

"What on earth are you all doing to me?" Getting me ready for the surgery I guess.

"God gives his hardest battles to his strongest soldiers."

DeMarcus Cousins

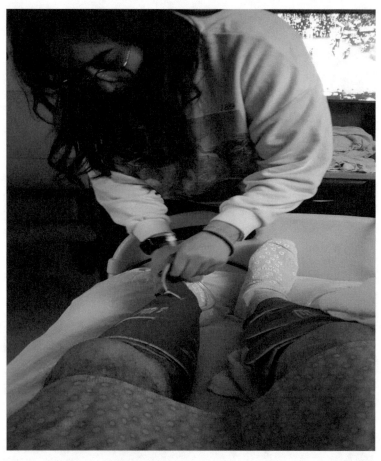

Meera making sure I don't get blood clots & getting me prepped for my walk.

"For I will restore health unto you, and I will heal you of your wounds, says the Lord." – Jeremiah 30:17a

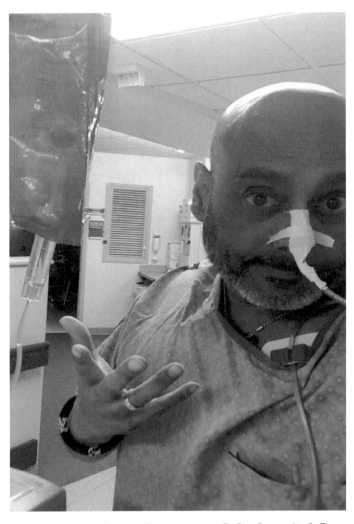

I was given a goal of 4 laps around the hospital floor. I
started with 8 and ended up doing 25 laps.

**"I have cancer. Cancer doesn't have
me." –Marco Calderon**

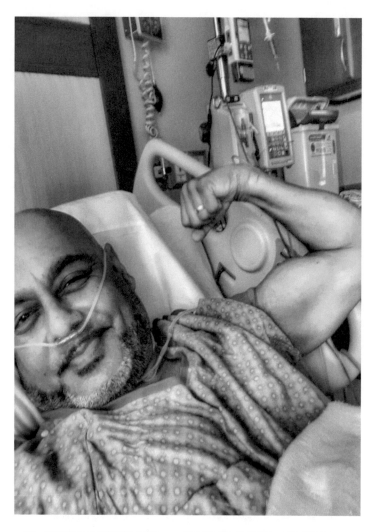

NEVER GIVE UP.

"You just can't beat the person who never gives up." – Babe Ruth

THANK YOU

I am forever grateful to the countless individuals who have lifted me up in prayer, supported me with their love and encouragement, and helped me navigate the challenges of colon cancer surgery. Your unwavering belief in me and your unrelenting support have been a beacon of hope and strength during this difficult journey. I am especially thankful to my dear friends and family, who have been my rock, my confidants, and my constant source of comfort. Your selflessness, kindness, and generosity have touched my heart in ways that words cannot express. I also extend my deepest gratitude to the exceptional medical team at Henry Ford Hospital, whose expertise, compassion, and care have been nothing short of remarkable. Your dedication to healing and your commitment to excellence have made a significant difference in my life, and I am forever in your debt. Thank you all for being instruments of hope, healing, and grace in my life. Your impact will never be forgotten.

Made in the USA
Columbia, SC
29 July 2024

39656085R00041